Lineberger Memorial

Library

Lutheran Theological Southern Seminary   Columbia, S. C.

The Delany Sisters

Reach High

The Delany Sisters
Reach High

ISBN 0-687-03074-9

Library of Congress Cataloging-in-Publication Data for The Delany Sisters REACH HIGH
is available from the Library of Congress.

02 03 04 05 06 07 08 09 10 11—10 9 8 7 6 5 4 3 2 1

Printed in Hong Kong

The Delany Sisters
Reach High

Written by Amy Hill Hearth
Illustrations by Tim Ladwig

Abingdon • Nashville

Dedication

For Sadie and Bessie, my cherished friends, who are remembered each day with love and affection.

—Amy Hill Hearth

Sarah Louise Delany was born September 19, 1889. She was calm and gentle. Her family nicknamed her "Sweet Sadie." Her little sister, Annie Elizabeth, was born two years later, on September 3, 1891. Bessie was just the opposite of Sadie. She was so bossy that she was called "Queen Bess."

The sisters, called Sadie and Bessie, both lived to be more than 100 years old. "We were best friends from day one," Bessie said. "Why, Sadie is in my earliest memory. I remember Papa called us into the house because a thunderstorm was coming. After the storm was over, there was the most beautiful rainbow. Sadie took my hand and we ran outside to get a better look at that rainbow. We thought God had hung it in the sky, just for us."

*S*adie and Bessie had eight brothers and sisters. They grew up in Raleigh, North Carolina, on the campus of Saint Augustine's College. Their mother was a teacher. Their father was a minister and vice-principal of the school.

"We had no money, but we were very happy," Sadie said. "We lived in buildings that belonged to the school. First we lived in a building called the Smith Building. When our family got too large, we moved to Delany Cottage. Saint Aug's was home!"

One day Bessie and Sadie asked Papa if they could have a nickel. They wanted to go to the soda fountain in downtown Raleigh. Bessie, Sadie, and their baby sister, Julia, held hands and formed a circle around Papa. "Papa, we are going to squeeze a nickel out of you," they said.

"Go ahead and try, daughters, but there's no nickel here!" Papa said, laughing.

Each morning all of the children had chores to do before breakfast. Sadie helped Mama prepare breakfast while Bessie supervised the younger children. Sadie liked being with Mama so much that she was called a "mama's child." "I was Mama's shadow," Sadie said. "Wherever Mama went, I was right there behind her."

Bessie preferred being in charge of the little ones. "I was a little dictator!" she said. "They used to complain to Mama that a gnat couldn't land on any of them without me knowing about it!"

*A*fter breakfast, all of the Delany children lined up for Papa's inspection before they left the house. "Papa wanted to make sure we looked proper," Sadie said. "He would look us over and make sure our clothes were neat, our ears and fingernails clean, and so on."

The sisters' parents were very proud of their children. Papa was born a slave. Mama was born free but very poor. Both Mama and Papa were college graduates and encouraged their children to "reach high." They wanted their children to work hard in school and aim for the stars.

Every morning the bells from the chapel would ring at eight o'clock. Papa would hurry out the door, with Mama, Sadie, Bessie, and the other children close behind. Papa had to be the first one at the chapel because he said morning prayers for the whole school. He built the chapel with his own hands in 1896, and it is still there today.

Sadie and Bessie went to school right on the campus of Saint Augustine's. They were taught by young teachers who were getting their training. Some of the students were grown-ups. They were former slaves who had not been allowed to learn to read and write when they were children. Bessie and Sadie and the other children shared their desks and textbooks with the old slaves.

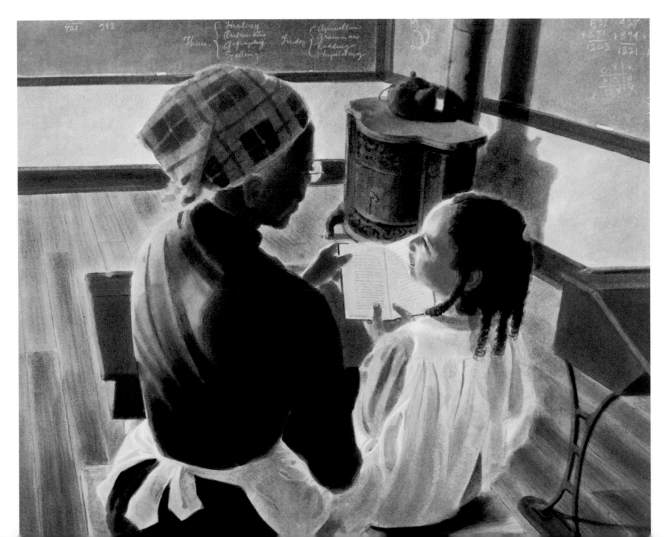

A lot of folks were very poor and in need of help. From time to time former slaves, mostly older men and women, would show up at the door. Mama always gave them a plate of food.

Mama always told them, "There's more where that came from." Sometimes they would eat two or three helpings.

One old fellow came and stayed for ten years, until the day he died. They called him "Uncle Jesse" and looked after him even though he was no kin to them. Another old man, Mr. Holloway, lived in an abandoned house nearby. Every Sunday Mama would pack up cake and whipped cream, and Sadie and Bessie would bring it to him, just to be friendly.

"Our parents thought it was their responsibility to treat these former slaves with dignity and kindness," Sadie said. "A lot of them were down on their luck. They'd been separated from their families and badly treated during slavery days. They'd never got used to being free."

Wherever the sisters went on campus, they liked to bring Bessie's pet pig, Retta. He was the runt of the litter, so weak and little that everyone thought he'd die. But Bessie took him and fed him with a bottle just like a baby. He grew up to be a big strong pig and followed the sisters around campus. Papa didn't like that. He didn't think it looked proper!

Sadie and Bessie loved to run through the fields surrounding the campus and pick wildflowers and berries. Sometimes they'd pick onions and eat them.

Papa didn't like that, either!

16

Mama and Papa were very protective. Sadie and Bessie were not allowed off campus without an adult to go with them. Usually that person was Culot, a cousin of Papa's who had been a slave. She worked as a seamstress at the school. She was an unmarried lady who was very attached to Sadie and Bessie. Sometimes they'd go into Raleigh for a treat. It took an hour to walk from campus. Even though she had very little money, Culot would buy a limeade or a piece of penny candy each for Sadie and Bessie.

There was a farm on campus which provided food and income for the school. The students who were very poor could work in the fields and make money for their expenses.

Bessie and Sadie loved to work at the farm to make a little money. Bessie was a champion cotton-picker. She always managed to pick more than Sadie.

"Culot always came along as our chaperone," Sadie said. "She would sit under a tree, with one eye on her sewing and the other eye on us—at the same time!"

On Sundays when the weather was nice, Mama would pack a picnic and the whole family would go to Pullen Park after church. The best part was that they got to take the trolley to get there. Sadie and Bessie loved to stand up front and let the breeze blow their hair.

One Sunday the conductor told them they could no longer sit up front. A new law had been passed, called the Jim Crow law. It meant that dark-skinned people had to sit in the back of the trolley. Only white people could sit up front.

Sadie and Bessie protested, but there was nothing that Papa could do. It was the law!

When they got to Pullen Park that Sunday, Bessie and Sadie helped Mama set up the picnic, then they ran to the well to get water.

"Look, Bessie!" Sadie said when they got to the well. Someone had put up a sign that read "White" on one side and "Colored" on the other. It was another one of those new Jim Crow laws!

Sadie felt like crying, but Bessie got mad. She took the dipper, scooped some water from the white side, and drank it! Sadie was scared Bessie would get in trouble, but she admired her little sister's courage. Several white people nearby looked angry, but Bessie didn't care.

*I*t was hard for Bessie and Sadie to understand why some white people didn't like them just because of the color of their skin. They knew some nice white people, like Miss Grace Moseley. She was a teacher they adored. Once a week, on Wednesday nights, Sadie and Bessie would go to Miss Moseley's place on campus. They would pile up on her big brass bed and Miss Moseley would read to them for hours, until they got sleepy. She liked to read classics, like Shakespeare.

Mama and Papa admired Miss Moseley. She was a well-educated lady from New England. Mama and Papa said education was the key to a good future. Reading, studying, and doing homework were part of every day except Sunday, which was the Lord's Day.

Sometimes, in the evenings after schoolwork and chores were done, the family got together in the living room for music. Every one of the children played an instrument, and as a family they formed a band. They had a small organ, a Mason & Hamlin, which Papa played beautifully. The girls took turns playing the organ, and the boys played trombone, clarinet, and violin. They loved to play marches, which were popular in the 1890's.

In the morning people would walk past the house and say, "Y'all had a party last night." It wasn't a party, it was just the family having fun.

"We lived a clean life, but Lord, we had a good time," said Bessie.

After the music time was over, it was bath time. Mama had to fill the tin tub in the kitchen ten times, once for each child!

"Mama always started with the youngest, and I was second-oldest, so I used to get so tired waiting for my turn," Sadie said. "It seemed like it took forever. I'd fall asleep waiting."

*A*fter each of the children had their bath, they joined the others in Papa's study. In their pajamas or nightgowns, they would gather around Papa, who would read Bible stories aloud.

Sometimes Papa would tell them about the day that the Civil War ended in 1865. This meant that the slaves were truly free. Papa was just seven years old. He said he ran about the house yelling, "Freedom! Freedom! I am free! I am free!"

After Papa was done talking to the children, he'd ask if anyone had an argument that day. "If any of us had a fuss that day, this is when we'd make up," Bessie said. "Papa didn't want his children mad at one another."

Then it was time for bed. The girls slept in one room and the boys slept in another. Everyone had his or her own little cot. Mama and Papa came to tuck in each child and hear their prayers, and kiss each child goodnight.

"We had a blessed childhood," Sadie said. "We had faith in the Lord. We had a lot of love and happiness and we carried that with us all of our lives."

Author's Note

Sadie and Bessie Delany graduated from Saint Augustine's School in Raleigh, North Carolina, and worked in the rural South as schoolteachers to earn money to continue their education. Sadie attended Columbia University and became a New York City public school teacher. In 1930 she became the first black person to teach domestic science on the high school level in New York City, a position previously reserved only for whites.

Bessie earned a Doctor of Dental Surgery degree from Columbia University in 1923. She was the second black woman licensed to practice dentistry in New York. She was well known as a dentist who accepted all patients, black or white, rich or poor.

The sisters never married, and lived together all their lives. They lived in Harlem and befriended many important black writers, artists, musicians, and intellectuals. Later, they lived in the Bronx, New York, while it was still partly rural. In 1957 they bought a house in Mount Vernon, New York, just north of New York City. In 1991, when Bessie turned 100 and Sadie turned 102, the sisters became famous when a young newspaper reporter from *The New York Times* wrote an article about them. Her name was Amy Hill Hearth. Mrs. Hearth and the sisters decided to collaborate on a full-length book, *Having Our Say: The Delany Sisters' First 100 Years,* published in 1993.

America was enchanted by the delightful Delany sisters! The book was a surprise bestseller, breaking records and winning many awards. In 1995, the book was adapted to the Broadway stage. A television film based on the book aired in 1999.

The sisters were deeply spiritual women. The lessons and prayers they learned in childhood were carried with them throughout their long lives.

Bessie Delany died on September 25, 1995, at the age of 104. Sadie Delany died four years later, on January 25, 1999, at the age of 109. They are buried beside their beloved parents in Raleigh, North Carolina. They are survived by several nieces and nephews, as well as friends, neighbors, and millions of admirers.